BUS FAYRE

Volume 14 Number 6   December 1991

MANAGING EDITOR: K. A. JENKINSON

BUS FAYRE is published by:

AUTOBUS REVIEW PUBLICATIONS LTD.,
42 Coniston Avenue, Queensbury, Bradford,
West Yorkshire BD13 2JD.

To take out a subscription to 'Bus Fayre' the cost is £20.00 per year (post paid) direct from the publishers. Subscriptions can commence with any issue and limited stocks of several back issues are also still available.

Notes, articles, reports and other original items printed in 'Bus Fayre' may not be reproduced either wholly or in part without the written permission of the publishers.

ISSN 0143 9162

The publishers of Bus Fayre are always pleased to accept manuscripts and/or photographs relating to the histories of coachbuilders and PSV chassis manufacturers for consideration for future publication. In particular we would welcome manuscripts and information concerning the lesser known manufacturers of both past and present times.

WE WISH
OUR READERS
A
HAPPY CHRISTMAS
AND
A
PROSPEROUS
NEW YEAR

Above: Amongst the most attractive double deck bodies built by Weymann were those of 4-bay construction built during the late 40s and 50s. Typifying this model is Bradford City Transport 34, an AEC Regent III of 1949 vintage which was further enhanced by its outswept skirt panels.

Front cover upper: Fitted with highbridge bodywork built to Weymann's classic early post-war design which owed much of its parentage to the Addlestone concern's products of the late 'thirties, this 1947 former Mansfield District AEC Regent II is now happily preserved as a reminder of Weymann's classic period. (P.T.Stokes)

Front cover lower: Also preserved is this AEC Reliance which was supplied new in 1955 to East Kent Road Car Co. Ltd. who are this year celebrating their 75th Anniversary. Its Weymann 41-seat dual purpose body incorporated numerous BET-Group design features.   (D.W.Rhodes)

Printed by Bakes & Lord Ltd., Beacon Road, Bradford BD6 3NB.

Distributed by SM Magazine Distribution Ltd.,
6 Leigham Court Road, Streatham, London
SW16 2PG. Tel: 081 677 8111

The history of WEYMANN

Part 2
1943 - 1965

Although Weymann had been forced to suspend the construction of bus bodywork in 1942 as a result of the continuation of the hostilities and turn their Addlestone factory over to essential war work, it was not long before the serious shortage of buses in many parts of war-torn Britain persuaded the Ministry of Supply to authorise a small number of bus bodybuilders and chassis manufacturers to resume production in order to alleviate this situation. Amongst the companies selected for this purpose was Weymann who were given authorisation to recommence the construction of double deck bus bodies early in 1943. These however had to be built to the Ministry's strictly laid down specifications and design and bore no resemblance to the bodies produced in the Addlestone factory during the period up to 1942. Of five bay, wood-framed construction, the 'utility' bodies incorporated none of the luxuries associated with Weymann's peacetime products and with their austere appearance, they looked extremely similar to the bodies built by some of the other 'authorised' builders at that time. Only one half-drop window to each side of each deck was permitted whilst inward-hinged ventilators were incorporated into their front upper deck bulkhead windows. Internally, these bodies were extremely spartan and with the lack of any trim panels, the body framework was visible to passengers. The single-skin roof had external ribs above each vertical body pillar and although a few bodies were fitted with leather-covered spring-filled seats, the majority of those built in 1943 had seats of the uncomfortable wooden slatted type. At first, all the Weymann 'utility' bodies were of highbridge construction with seating for 56 passengers and were mounted on Guy Arab or Daimler CWA6 chassis and it was not until 1944 that any 55-seat lowbridge bodies were built. By this time, only Guy Arab chassis were being supplied to the Addlestone factory and thus no further Daimlers were bodied to MoS specification.

Prior to Weymann's re-entry into the field of bus body construction in

1943 however, the Ministry of War Transport had during the previous year diverted 15 Sunbeam MF2 chassis, which had been built for export to Johannesburg, South Africa, to Bradford Corporation (10) and Nottingham City Transport (5) and authorised the Addlestone concern to build the bodies for these. As they were 8ft. in width, special

Amongst the first austere wartime bodies to be built by Weymann were ten on Sunbeam MF2 trolleybus chassis which were unable to be shipped to their original buyer in Johannesburg due to the escalation of the war. Unusual in being of 8ft. width, these were delivered to Bradford Corporation in 1942 with 5 similar trolleybuses going to Nottingham. Seen here when new, Bradford 698 although surprisingly delivered in peacetime livery, has anti-splinter mesh fitted to its windows and its wings and guard rails painted white.

Pictured shortly after its entry into service in 1944 with its wing tips and guard rails painted white, Birmingham Corporation Guy Arab II had only one half-drop window to each side of its upper and lower decks and had inward-hinged ventilators incorporated into its front upper deck bulkhead windows.

The gas lamp and old-style buildings give a vintage flavour to this picture of one of Midland Red's Weymann-bodied Guy Arab IIs built in 1944.

Fitted with lowbridge Weymann bodywork built to the design and specification laid down by the MoS, East Kent Guy Arab II BJG421 was new in 1945 and despite having additional half-drop side windows, was fitted with inward-hinged ventilators in its upper deck front bulkhead.

New to Southdown in 1945, this Guy Arab II seen here after its sale to Llandudno & Colwyn Bay Electric Railway Co. was fitted with Weymann's relaxed style of MoS specification bodywork which was given additional half-drop side windows and fixed glazing to its front upper deck bulkhead.

authorisation had to be gained for their operation in Britain and, after this had been granted, Weymann built highbridge, full-fronted bodies to the MoS specification which was to become standard for the remainder of the war years.

Although the majority of the utility bodies built by Weymann were of composite construction, a tiny number were built on metal frames and fitted mainly on Guy Arab chassis during 1944/5, the only exceptions being two mounted on Daimler CWA6 chassis for Maidstone & District and Glasgow Corporation in 1944. Whilst retaining the same basic styling as the composite utility bodies, the all-metal variants incorporated pan-mounted windows which featured radiused lower corners and as such, looked slightly more attractive. All but two were of highbridge configuration with seating for 56 passengers, the odd men out being 48-seat lowbridge bodies for Aldershot & District in 1945.

During the early part of 1945, with the prospect of peace being in sight, the Ministry of Supply relaxed slightly their rigid specification to allow more opening windows to be incorporated into the wartime bodies being built by several manufacturers and immediately Weymann took advantage of this and at the same time, resulting from the extra ventilation being permitted through half-drop side windows, offered bodies with fixed glazing to the upper deck front bulkhead, thus eliminating the inward-hinged ventilators.

Later in 1945, Weymann began to look ahead to normal peacetime

Weymann introduced its new post-war double deck body at the end of 1945. Based on the design launched before the outbreak of World War II, it was of highbridge configuration and had a classic appearance, this being helped by its outswept lower panels. Mounted on an AEC Regent II chassis and new in 1946, this example (GRR345) was supplied to Mansfield District Traction Co.

One of the Weymann highbridge-bodied AEC Regent IIs purchased by South Wales Transport in 1946, 276 although having metal weather louvres over its front upper deck bulkhead windows only had these fitted above the opening windows along each side of its upper and lower saloons, this giving the impression of deeper side windows and greater overall height.

For their prototype home-built D1-type chassis, Midland Red designed their own double deck body and contracted Weymann to build this in 1945. Surprisingly however, HHA1 remained unique as Midland Red placed their orders for production bodies of this style with other coachbuilders rather than Weymann who built no further bodies for this operator until the 'sixties.

production and to this end set about designing new double and single deck bodies which could be offered on the open market. For double deckers, the design evolved was heavily based on that of classic appearance used in 1940. Of 5-bay construction, it had a pleasing smooth curved front and employed Weymann's distinctive style of front upper deck windows which had radiused outer top corners. All the remaining windows, some of which incorporated half-drop ventilators, had radiused lower corners whilst a full-length metal weather louvre could be fitted or merely affixed above the opening windows. A choice of inswept or outswept lower panels was available and although internally this new style of body was fitted with the customary trim panels, it retained a single skin roof which featured external ribs. The first of these new bodies made their debut in December 1945 mounted on AEC Regent II chassis.

Although regarded as a standard body, thirty of these new double deckers were supplied to Liverpool Corporation in an unfinished state for completion by that municipality in their own Edge Lane workshops, thus reviving memories of pre-war years when this undertaking had similarly completed a number of Weymann bodies.

Despite immediately starting to build a standard product as soon as the dark years of war had ended, Weymann in 1945 also undertook the contruction of a new all-metal double deck body for Midland Red to that operator's own design. This was of four bay configuration and featured an attractively-curved front and rear and had an open rear platform. The side windows to each deck were radiused at all four corners with some incorporating sliding ventilators while the base of the front upper deck bulkhead windows curved upwards to the centre pillar to match the upward curve of the moulding at upper deck floor level. A neat full-width bonnet and concealed radiator did much to enhance the appearance of this attractive body which was mounted on a home-built Midland Red chassis. Surprisingly however, when Midland Red took the decision to order more bodies of this design for delivery on

Amongst the first post-war lowbridge bodies to be built at Addlestone were a number supplied on Leyland PD1 chassis to Chesterfield Corporation in 1947. One of these, JRA 638 shows the classic lines of Weymann's standard 5-bay body with its distinctive upper deck front bulkhead windows etc.

AEC Regent II chassis in 1948/9, the contract was given to Brush rather than Weymann and thus this body remained unique.

Another feature of the ending of the hostilities was the speed with which Weymann began to re-establish themselves in the export market when in 1946 they supplied double deck highbridge bodies (of British standard design except for the fitting of additional opening windows) on Daimler CVG6 chassis to Cape Electric Tramways, Capetown; Pietermaritzburg; Port Elizabeth; Johannesburg and Pretoria, South Africa. Six half-cab 32-seat dual door single deck bodies on AEC Regal chassis were also supplied to Lisbon Electric Tramways, Portugal at this same time.

Meanwhile, back on the home front, Weymann's new standard double deck body in its highbridge form, whilst more usually being fitted with seating for 30 passengers in the upper deck

Weymann's first RT-type bodies built for London Transport to that undertaking's own design and specification featured a route number box in their front roof dome as illustrated by RT439, a 1947 example.

Looking superb is Brighton Corporation 83, a 1947 AEC Regent III with Weymann standard 4-bay metal-framed body. Having outswept skirt panels, half-drop side windows and ventilators incorporated into its front upper deck bulkhead windows, its styling was a true classic in its time.

Typifying Weymann's first post-war single deck design is Sheffield Corporation 53, an AEC Regal I of 1948 vintage. Its forward-projecting roof and angled bulbous dash panel gave it a frowning appearance in contrast to its outswept lower panels.

BUS FAYRE 167

Mounted on a Leyland PS1 chassis, this 1948 bus of Hebble Motor Services was given Weymann bodywork built to BET styling which featured a forward projecting front roof dome and porch-type rear entrance.

and 26 in the lower saloon could be modified to meet particular operators demands and to this end Kingston upon Hull Corporation specified a slightly different seating arrangement with 31 on the upper deck and 29 in the lower saloon. Although the majority of Weymann's new highbridge bodies built in 1946 were fitted to AEC Regent II chassis, Maidstone & District mounted these on Bristol K6A chassis (and one on a K6B chassis) while Luton Corporation also utilised the Bristol K6A chassis. A lowbridge version of Weymann's standard post war body also made its debut towards the end of 1946 when a number of 53-seat examples on Leyland PD1 chassis were supplied to Chesterfield Corporation.

A 5-bay lowbridge body of Weymann's standard post-war design is illustrated here on City of Oxford 137, an AEC Regent III of 1949 vintage. With inswept side panels, this bus also lacked weather louvres above the windows on each deck. (T.G. Walker)

One of 100 AEC Regent IIIs placed in service by Liverpool Corporation in 1948/9 fitted with Weymann bodies completed by that municipality in its Edge Lane works, A572 like its sisters, featured a more upright front than was used by Weymann on its standard bodies.

Trolleybuses continued to be bodied by Weymann throughout the post-war period and in 1949 a batch of BUT 9611Ts were thus treated for Notts & Derby. Employing the Addlestone concern's classic 5-bay styling, these additionally had twin ventilators fitted to their front roof domes on pre-war fashion. NNU237, along with its sisters was, upon the closure of the Notts & Derby system sold for further service to Bradford City Transport, with whom it is seen here.

168 BUS FAYRE

Only three British operators specified Weymann metal framed half cab bodywork during the post-war period. One of these was Crosville whose 1950 Leyland PS1 KA258 is pictured here in its owner's all-cream coach livery.

The first metal-framed single deck bodies built by Weymann for the home market in post-war years were of BET styling and when fitted to the AEC Regal III chassis, featured the same windscreen and mouldings as used on Weymann's standard double deck bodies of the period. This example was one of a number fitted with dual purpose-type seating supplied to Mansfield District in 1950.

On the single deck front, except for the six bodies built for Lisbon, Portugal, all those built at the Addlestone factory were of composite construction and were based on the BET's standard design similar in many ways to that produced immediately before the outbreak of war. Either front or rear entrance configuration could be specified, the entrance itself being of the porch type and in the case of those supplied to London Transport, no door was fitted to the passenger entrance to conform to legislation laid down by the Metropolitan Police. With radiused lower corners to their windows, some of which incorporated sliding ventilators, and outswept lower panels, these bodies looked most attractive and could be easily recognised by the full width front roof dome which protruded forward above the windscreen to give a 'frowning' appearance. Those bodies fitted to AEC Regal chassis had a slightly angled windscreen below which the front dash protruded forward in similar fashion to that of pre-war years while the bodies fitted to Leyland PS1 chassis omitted this feature and instead had a smoother frontal appearance. The emergency exit was more usually positioned at the offside front immediately aft of the cab door, although it could be optionally located behind the rear axle.

During 1947, Weymann's standard double deck body underwent a minor 'face-lift' particularly in the area of the windscreen which was replaced by one of a slightly greater depth below which was added a revised moulding and at this same time a four-bay version of this style of body was also made available. As an alternative to half-drop windows, sliding ventilators could be specified and a sliding cab door was offered as an option to the previous hinged type. Both high and low bridge versions of the 'new' body were available and could be mounted on any make of chassis. Internally, these bodies were finished to a high standard and incorporated polished wood trim around the windows in almost pre-war fashion.

The lowbridge version of Weymann's standard double deck body on Midland General's 1950 AEC Regent III 422 had sliding ventilators fitted to its side windows and half-drop windows to its front upper deck bulkhead above which were twin scoop-ventilators reminiscent of pre-war years.

BUS FAYRE 169

Bournemouth Corporation favoured full-fronted bodywork for its double deckers and specified this feature on its 1950 Leyland PD2/3s which additionally had twin staircases and were of dual-door layout. One of these, 123 is seen here in its home town in company with others of its type and a Weymann Aurora-bodied Leyland PD3.

Further orders from overseas customers were received from Lisbon Electric Tramways, Portugal for no fewer than 42 half-cab single deck 24-seat dual door bodies of all-metal construction on AEC Regal III chassis and from Salisbury United Omnibus Co., Southern Rhodesia for 12 39-seat front entrance bodies on Daimler CVG5 chassis, and all of these were delivered during 1948.

Prior to this, Weymann had become involved in London Transport's massive bus replacement programme and had accepted contracts to build a large quantity of that undertaking's new RT-type bodies. These had been designed by London Transport in

Based on Weymann's standard post-war double deck design, Bournemouth Corporation's 3-axle BUT 9641T trolleybus 256 had two-door bodywork with twin staircases and was new in 1950. Enhanced by its operator's predominantly primrose livery, it looks majestic as it stands in company with one of its sisters in the centre of its home town.

Following their earlier practise of building bodies to operator's own specification, Weymann in 1948 built 100 highbridge double deck bodies on AEC Regent III chassis for Liverpool Corporation. Whilst these bore much resemblance to Weymann's standard 4-bay design, they featured a more vertical front and had inswept lower panels, thus giving them a noticably different overall appearance.

Although purchasing standard bodies from Weymann on Leyland PD1 chassis during the latter months of 1947 and early part of 1948, Plymouth Corporation only received three of these complete and ready for service, the remainder being ordered in frame form for completion in their own workshops (12) or by local coachbuilder Mumford (10).

Although most of Weymann's body production was for fitting to motor bus chassis, the trolleybus was not neglected and in 1947, six bodies were built for South Lancashire Transport on three-axle Karrier MS2 chassis. These were of highbridge configuration and had seating for 34 passengers in their upper saloon and 30 in the lower deck. During the following year, six conventional 54-seat bodies were built on BUT 9611T chassis for Brighton Corporation and six with seating for 56 passengers on BUT 9611T chassis for neighbouring Brighton, Hove & District while for the export market three single deck trolleybus bodies on BUT 9712T chassis were constructed for Sao Paulo, Brazil.

The onlt single deck BUT RETB1 trolleybus to be bodied by Weymann was this dual door example for Glasgow Corporation which was new in 1951.

170 BUS FAYRE

The first Weymann bodies to be built on underfloor-engined chassis were delivered to Western Welsh in 1951 on Leyland Royal Tiger chassis. One of these, FUH423 shows the original styling of the Hermes body with shallow windscreens and advert panel above its side windows.

Built in 1952 on a Leyland PD2/12 chassis for Southport Corporation, the body on this bus was to Weymann's revised standard 5-bay design with rubber-mounted side windows, inswept side panels and sliding cab door.

During the early 'fifties, Maidstone & District despatched a number of its wartime and pre-war buses to Addlestone to be fitted with new Weymann bodies. Amongst these was DH71, a wartime Guy which in 1952 was given this attractive highbridge body of revised 5-bay design with rubber-mounted windows, outswept side panels and a sliding door to the driver's cab.

During 1948, the RT-type bodies built for London Transport were updated by the elimination of the roof-mounted route number box and the fitting of a revised three-apperture destination screen as illustrated by Country Area RT3814 which made its debut in 1953.

pre-war days and closely resembled those built by that concern in its Chiswick body shop on specially-modified AEC Regent chassis during the 1939/40 period. Of four bay construction, the first of the new generation of RT bodies built by Weymann and Park Royal were completed during 1947 and featured a front, roof mounted route number box, although unlike the pre-war bodies of this style, this was omitted from the rear roof dome. In the autumn of 1948 the body was slightly restyled to eliminate this front roof-mounted feature when the normal destination screen was redesigned as a three, rather than a two apperture unit. Seating was provided for 56 passengers and the interior was finished to London Transport's own

Dating from 1953, this lowbridge Weymann-bodied AEC Regent III of South Wales Transport had rubber-mounted windows and an unglazed additional panel to the rear of the lower deck, thus signifying its 27ft. length.

specification and made use of vinyl covered window surrounds as well as side panels.

In 1949/50, Liverpool Corporation took delivery of a further 140 bodies on Daimler CVA6 and AEC Regent III chassis to the same almost vertical front design as those supplied in 1948, receiving them in frame form for completion locally. Whilst the 40 bodies on Daimler CVA chassis were finished in the Corporation's own workshops during 1948, the 100 AEC Regent IIIs received in 1949 proved to be too numerous for the municipality to complete themselves. This resulted in 39 being finished in their own Edge Lane works, 10 being despatched to Pearson, a local coachbuilder for completion, 10 to Davidsons, 20 to Aero Engineering and 21 to Blakes for finishing.

Notts & Derby took 15 Weymann-bodied BUT 9611T trolleybuses into stock in 1949 while Liverpool Corporation completed a solitary body of their own vertical-front type and fitted this to the prototype 7.7 litre-engined AEC Regent III chassis. More bodies were built for overseas customers during 1949 when 5 standard design 56-seat highbridge AEC Regent IIIs were despatched to City of East London, South Africa and more unusually, 20 highbridge 64-seat bodies on 3-axle Daimler CVG6 chassis were supplied to Cape Electric Tramways, Cape Town. City of East London also at this same time took delivery of 15 all-metal 39-seat front entrance single deck bodies on AEC Regal III and Daimler CVG5 chassis while a 37-seat dual door all-metal body on an AEC Regal III chassis was exported to South America for demonstration purposes and 4 bodies were sent to Germiston in shell form for completion locally.

Liverpool Corporation purchased 60 Weymann-bodied Leyland PD2/12s in 1953, the bodies of which were modified to incorporate styling features specified by their operator. One of these buses, L22, clearly shows the revised frontal design associated with these vehicles.

A pair of Glasgow Corporation's Weymann-bodied Sunbeam trolleybuses of 1953 vintage stand at Hampden depot and show the traditional styling of their 'standard' bodies.

One of only two Weymann Hermes bodies to be built with a Scottish-style cut-away rear entrance, Sheffield Corporation 223, a Leyland Royal Tiger, was new in 1953.

The first metal-framed single deck bodies to be built by Weymann for home operators made their debut in 1949 when a number were constructed on AEC Regal III chassis for Mansfield District Traction Co. Employing many features associated with BET-style bodies, these bore some resemblance to Weymann's composite single deck bodies except that they had windows of slightly greater length, inswept lower panels and featured a full width front canopy which did not protrude forward of the windscreen. A more vertical cab was incorporated into the design and the windscreen and front dash panel was the same as that used on Weymann's standard double deck design of the period, giving the finished product a far more handsome appearance than that of its composite predecessor. Having a front, porch-style entrance, its emergency exit was located immediately behind the driver's cab door and dual purpose-type seating was provided for 35 passengers. A number of bodies of this new style were also built on Leyland PS1/1 chassis in 1950 for Crosville whilst in this same year Birmingham City Transport took delivery of 30 of these bodies on Leyland PS2/1 chassis, fitting these with 34 bus-type seats.

Taking advantage of the new legislation which allowed double deck buses to be 27ft. rather than 26ft. in overall length, Weymann began to build bodies to this increased dimension in 1950, basing these on their standard design. Both 4 and 5-bay variants were available and on the former a small, unglazed panel was added behind the rearmost lower deck side window to compensate for the extra length without the need to increase the dimensions of the side windows. Given the extra 12 inches internally, this enabled the seating capacity to be increased from 56 to 59 passengers (31 in the upper saloon, 28 in the lower deck) and amongst the first operators to take advantage of this was Rochdale Corporation who

Fitted with lowbridge Weymann Aurora 5-bay bodywork fitted with rear platform doors, South Wales Transport 1181, an AEC Regent III with wide bonnet and concealed radiator was new in 1954.

The deep side windows of the 5-bay Aurora body fitted in 1954 to Maidstone & District's wartime Bristol K6A DH115 gives it a handsome appearance even if this was not regarded by some to be as attractive as Weymann's earlier post-war double deck design.

BUS FAYRE 173

One of Weymann's most loyal overseas customers was Lisbon Electric Tramways, Portugal who purchased a number of batches of both double and single deck bodies during the 1940s and 1950s. One of these buses, standard-bodied AEC Regent III 255 (BB-21-07) has now been preserved in England and is seen here soon after its return to the country in which it was built in 1955. (T.W.W.Knowles)

took 10 bodies on AEC Regent III chassis. Meanwhile, Bournemouth Corporation who, during the late 1930s, had favoured full-fronted bodies for their Leyland TD5 double deckers, ordered 30 bodies of this styling for delivery in 1951 on Leyland PD2/3 chassis. In addition to having full-width cabs, these featured concealed radiators and were of dual-door, twin staircase layout with an open rear platform and a narrow exit, protected by a driver-controlled folding door, immediately behind the

The only Routemaster body to be produced by Weymann was that of prototype Leyland-engined RML3 which was completed during the early spring of 1956. Built to London Transport's own design and specification it differed from the earlier two buses of this type by having a narrower bonnet.

Western Welsh 1233, new in 1956 was a Weymann integrally-constructed Leyland Olympian which outwardly bore a strong resemblance to Weymann's Hermes single deckers and incorporated BET styling.

front bulkhead. Seating on these buses was provided for 48 passengers of which 27 were accommodated in the upper saloon. Bournemouth also took delivery in 1950 of 24 dual door 56-seat double deck bodies on 3-axle BUT 9641T trolleybus chassis, these being almost identical to the motorbus bodies supplied to this municipality except for their extra length.

The export market continued to play an important role for Weymann and in 1950 a further 6 double deck bodies on AEC Regent III chassis were supplied to Lisbon Electric Tramways, Portugal. During the following year, 20 highbridge 56-seat bodies on BUT 9611T trolleybus chassis were despatched to Colombo Municipal Passenger Transport, Ceylon and 10 highbridge 62-seat bodies on Guy Arab III chassis to Lahore Regional Transport Board, Pakistan while a 41-seat dual door single deck body on a BUT LETB1 trolleybus chassis was exported to Empresa Municipal de Transportes in Madrid. 9 single deck all-metal bodies on Leyland chassis were built for A.M.D.E.T., Montevideo, Uruguay in 1950 while 90 bodies were supplied in ckd or frame form to South Africa for assembly by Bus Bodies (South Africa) Ltd. and other local coachbuilding concerns.

Back home, 1951 witnessed the construction of a single deck body on a BUT RETB1 trolleybus chassis for

New in 1956, this 27ft. long Gardner-engined AEC Regent V of Rochdale Corporation shows the additional small window added to the rear of the lower deck to compensate for the extra body length without the need to increase the length of the otherwise-standard rubber mounted side windows.

Kingston upon Hull City Transport specified dual-door layout for its 1961 Weymann Hermes-bodied AEC Reliances, the exit of which was located immediately in front of the rear wheel arch.

BUS FAYRE 175

Illustrating Weymann's lowbridge Aurora body with rear platform doors is this 1957 Leyland PD3/4 of East Midland.

Previous page:

The classic lines of Weymann's standard post-war double deck body design are captured by this lowbridge example on an AEC Regent III chassis. New in 1950 to London Transport for country area duties, KYY506 later served in the fleet of Leeds independent, Samuel Ledgard in whose blue & grey livery it is seen here in Otley in 1965.

Dating from 1958, this 43-seat AEC Reliance of Aldershot & District employed BET styling but had flat windscreens which were not inward raked towards their top edge.

Mounted on a Leyland Worldmaster chassis, the BET-style Hermes body on Halifax Corporation 2 (KCP2) was of the revised styling with slightly deeper windscreens. It was new in 1958.

Glasgow Corporation. This was of standee layout with seating for only 26 passengers and had jack-knife doors located forward of the front axle and aft of the rear wheel arch. Given an unusually deep roof, small additional windows were fitted above the normal side windows - each of which had a radii to all four corners and some of which incorporated sliding ventilators - for the benefit of standing passengers whilst at the front, deep rearward angled twin windscreens gave the body a pleasant appearance. Apart from the body built on the LETB1 chassis for Madrid - which had its passenger doors on the offside - no further bodies of this styling were built.

Following the advent of underfloor-engined chassis for single deck use, Weymann evolved a new body for this purpose, basing its design on that specified by the B.E.T. Group. This had seating for 44 passengers and had its passenger entrance - which was fitted with a jack-knife door - located forward of the front axle, adjacent to the driver, thus making it eminently suitable for one-person-operation.

Employing a straight waist rail which was stepped downwards slightly forward of the front wheel arch, it had rubber-mounted windows, all four corners of which were radiused, which incorporated sliding ventilators. The nicely-curved roof had its edges flattened to allow adverts to be carried above the side windows whilst the emergency exit was positioned in the centre of the rear bulkhead. At the front, the twin, flat windscreens were

New to Rhondda in 1958, this Weymann Fanfare-bodied Leyland Tiger Cub was fitted with sliding ventilators to its side windows. The style of mouldings used by Weymann further enhanced this attractive design which was also available to overseas customers under the name Arcadian.

angled inward towards their top edge to reduce glare, although the outer corner pillars remained almost vertical. The first of these new-style bodies, which were given the name 'Hermes', were fitted to Leyland Royal Tiger chassis and were supplied to Western Welsh during 1951. Later in the year, a second version of the Hermes was produced with a porch-style rear entrance and seating for 42 passengers, the first examples of which were mounted on underfloor-engined Atkinson chassis for North Western Road Car Co. Ltd. For the export market, a ckd version of the Hermes was produced under the name 'Jason'.

Although much of Weymann's production was concentrated on its 'standard' designs, the Addlestone factory remained willing to build bodies to operator's own specifications whenever this was required and in 1952 constructed a number of 4-bay 56-seat double deck bodies for Liverpool Corporation. Unlike the previous Weymann bodies built for this municipality, these were only loosely- based on their manufacturer's standard design and had a more rounded rear roof dome and rubber-mounted windows with radii to all four corners. The front upper deck bulkhead windows incorporated push-out ventilators and omitted Weymann's distinctive heavy radii to their outer top corners. Mounted on Leyland PD2/12 chassis, these buses were of 8ft. width and had inswept

Despite their close ties with Metropolitan Cammell Carriage & Wagon Co. Ltd. through their joint marketing organisation, MCW, Weymann had until now evolved its own designs and had not emulated those produced by MCCW at its Elmdon works, although such bodies as the Hermes which was built to BET design and specification was common to both companies, albeit with minor differences. From the early 'fifties however, much closer co-operation between the Addlestone and Elmdon factories became noticable and a number of the new designs had more than just a similarity in their appearance.

1952 saw the introduction of a new double deck body which was lighter in weight than Weymann's previous bodies and made use of glassfibre for such items as roof domes and corner panels etc. Of highbridge configuration, this new body which was given the name 'Aurora' was of

All the trolleybuses purchased new by Bournemouth Corporation since 1934 had been fitted with a rear open platform entrance and front exit door. This 63-seat Weymann-bodied Sunbeam MF2B of 1958 vintage had its front exit placed forward of its front axle.

Carrying Aurora 4-bay bodywork, this Leyland PD2/37 of Brighton Corporation was new in 1959 and features the scoop-type ventilator in its front roof dome that was to become a common feature on bodies of this style.

The attractive styling of Weymann's first post-war coach body, the Fanfare, can be seen from this view of Southdown 1137, a 1959 Leyland Tiger Cub with Auster-type ventilators incorporated into its side windows.

During the late 'fifties and early 'sixties, Weymann's Aurora body was available in either rear or front entrance configuration. One of the latter on an AEC Regent V chassis is seen here numbered 529 in the fleet of South Wales Transport with whom it entered service in 1959.

5-bay construction and had deep rubber-mounted windows to each deck, some of which incorporated sliding ventilators. The glassfibre front roof dome unit extended to the base of the upper deck windows and resulted in thick corner pillars being employed, thus giving the Aurora body a distinctive appearance. MCCW also launched an almost identical body under the name 'Orion' at this same time. A further new body to be introduced by Weymann was a single decker named the 'Apollo' designed for use in Beunos Aires, Argentina. 100 such bodies were supplied on Leyland Royal Tiger chassis during 1952/3.

Meanwhile, in 1951 Weymann had updated its 'standard' all-metal body by fitting it with rubber-mounted windows with all corners radiused and replacing the original style divided emergency exit window in the upper deck rear bulkhead with a single-piece glazed unit. An optional feature on this revised body was a curved nearside front panel beneath the canopy which swept forward towards the front wing. Both 4 and 5-bay variants continued to be available and the lower panels could be in or out-swept depending on customers preferences.

Throughout the early 1950s, Weymann, in addition to building bodies for mounting on new chassis, also produced a quantity for fitting to pre-war or wartime chassis to give them an extended lease of life. Almost all were double deckers, with Maidstone & District and Devon General being amongst the major customers in this particular field. The bodies ordered by the latter were of lightweight construction and were used on rebuilt pre-war AEC Regal chassis. Lisbon Electric Tramways also purchased 2 'standard' bodies for fitting to a pair of former single deck AEC Regal III chassis during 1952, although these were supplied in kit form for local assembly in Portugal whereas the 25 bodies built for that operator on new AEC Regent III chassis were delivered complete and were followed by a further 11 in 1953.

1953 saw more Weymann double deck bodies delivered on Leyland PD2/12 chassis to Liverpool

Amongst the last Hermes 30ft. long bodies to be built by Weymann was a number supplied to Edinburgh Corporation in 1961 on Leyland Tiger Cub chassis. Featuring the latest style of ventilators to its side windows and a raised waistrail, 99 is seen here on a private hire duty when still quite new.

180 BUS FAYRE

The rear entrance highbridge Aurora body is typified by this Chesterfield Corporation Leyland PD2/30 built in 1960 and fitted with ventilators to its upper deck front bulkhead windows and given a sliding door to the driver's cab.

Corporation to that undertaking's own specification while Glasgow Corporation received a batch of fifteen Sunbeam F4A trolleybuses with Weymann 62-seat bodies. These were built largely to the Addlestone concern's 'standard' design and bore many traditional Weymann features.

The export market continued to play an important role in Weymann's fortunes and in 1954 a total of 45 single deck bodies were built on Leyland Royal Tiger chassis for Chile. Unfortunately however, after the first 20 had been despatched to their purchaser, the remainder of the order was cancelled, leaving 23 completed vehicles to be placed in store until a new customer could be found, the final two having not yet been built. Eventually, in 1955, these buses finally left Addlestone to join Empresa, Madrid (15), C.O.P.S.A., Uraguay (4), Kuwait (1), Yugoslavia (1), Venezuela (1) and Damascus (1). Several Leyland Tiger Cubs with Weymann bodywork were exported to Trinidad in 1954/5 while in 1954 21 single deck-bodied Leylands were built for Jamaica Omnibus Service.

Back on the home market, 1954 saw the introduction of Weymann's first full luxury coach body in post-war years, this being christened the 'Fanfare' and being of attractive styling. Using a waistrail which curved gently downwards towards the rear, its foremost side window was D-shaped whilst the window in the passenger door forward of the front

Typifying the lowheight bodywork built by Weymann for fitting to the rear-engined Leyland Atlantean chassis, PMT L870 of 1961 vintage was additionally fitted with an illuminated advertising panel to its offside.

One of Weymann's less-pleasing designs was that evolved jointly with Western Welsh for fitting to AEC Reliance chassis for that company in 1960/1. Its windscreens did little to enhance its appearance and its slab sides with minimum moulding added to its ugly styling. Fortunately, only 12 such bodies - named the Cambrian class by their operator - were built and initially all these coaches were employed on touring duties.

BUS FAYRE 181

Although wearing bus livery, this 1961 Weymann-bodied Albion Nimbus of Western Welsh was fitted from new with 30 coach-type seats. As can be seen from its styling, its body incorporated numerous BET features and overall gave the look of a conventional-sized vehicle.

One of a number of Weymann-bodied Leyland Atlantean PDR1/1s purchased by East Midland in 1961, D152 had ventilators incorporated into its front upper deck bulkhead windows and nearside windscreen.

axle and driver's offside windows were of the same shape reversed. The entrance door was of the inward-hinged type and incorporated a window towards its lower edge while at the front, the twin deep raked windscreens were flanked by curved corner glazing to give a distinctive appearance. Below the windscreens the vertical dash panel projected slightly forward and to give additional natural light to the interior of the body, two glazed panels were incorporated into the front roof dome. Internally the body was luxuriously appointed and could accommodate 37 - 41 passengers, and externally, polished mouldings towards the lower edge of the panels gave the Fanfare a distinctive appearance. The emergency exit was positioned in the centre of the offside.

Meanwhile, in 1954, although the single deck BET-style Hermes body continued in production without any major change except for the fitting of rounded, rather than flat-type cant panels, two bodies were built on Leyland Royal Tiger chassis for Sheffield Corporation which featured a Scottish-style cut-away rear entrance

A unique vehicle, this coach-seated Bristol LHS6L which began life with Western Welsh in 1968 was fitted from new with a Weymann body removed from one of its operator's 1961 Albion Nimbus vehicles.

Weymann's Castilian coach body was less attractive than that of its predecessor, the Fanfare and incorporated a shallower roof dome and revised windscreen layout in addition to having longer, if not as attractive, side windows. One of Southdown's Castilian-bodied Leyland Leopards of 1963 vintage, 1169 is seen here on an express journey from London to Worthing soon after its entry into service.

and had seating for 31 passengers. A further variant was built for Lancashire United Transport on Guy Arab UF chassis which had flat windscreens which were not angled inward towards their top edge and the base of which curved upwards towards the centre pillar.

1955/6 saw the purchase of a large number of double deck bodies to Glasgow Corporation on Daimler CVG6, AEC Regent V and Leyland PD2/25 chassis and while 85 of these were delivered complete, 74 were supplied as sets of materials to W.Alexander & Son Ltd. of Falkirk for construction in that coachbuilder's factory. Similarly, during 1956/7 Weymann provided Glasgow Corporation with the frames for 20 single deck Hermes-type dual door 40-seat bus bodies which were assembled by the Corporation in its own Coplawhill car works and mounted on Leyland Worldmaster RT3/1 chassis.

During 1956, the BET-style Hermes single deck body underwent minor restyling when it was given slightly deeper windscreens which in turn caused the waistrail to be stepped down further at the front. A dual door variant was also introduced with doors located forward of the front and rear axles while either inward angled or flat windscreens could now be specified. For the export market, a new coach body almost identical to the Fanfare was launched under the name 'Arcadian', the main difference from the Fanfare being the incorporation of full air conditioning into its body.

Having completed its last RT-type bodies for London Transport in 1954, Weymann were delighted when they were asked to build the body for one of the prototypes of London's new generation of double deckers, the Routemaster. This was completed in the early spring of 1956 - although it was not taken into London Transport stock until the first day of July 1957 - and was constructed to its operator's own design and specification. Of 4-bay configuration with an open rear platform and seating for 64 passengers,, the Routemaster was integrally built and employed two separate running units which were attached directly to the body underframe. The Weymann-built example was fitted with a Leyland engine and, originally numbered RML3 differed from the two earlier prototypes in having a narrower bonnet and radiator grille (which was modified later during its life). Unfortunately however, despite completing this vehicle, no further Routemasters were built at Addlestone as a result of London Transport placing the contract for all the production vehicles exclusively with Park Royal Coachworks.

Meanwhile, towards the end of 1957, the long-established and ever popular standard double deck design was discontinued in favour of the Aurora, of which a lowbridge version had been introduced in 1954 and a front entrance variant in 1957. Although both these were of 5-bay construction, during 1958 a 4-bay version was added to the range, thus extending customer's options even further.

The next new model to emerge from the Addlestone factory was the Leyland Olympian single decker, an integrally-constructed bus which closely resembled the Hermes and was built to BET specification despite it being designed jointly by Leyland, MCCW and Weymann. Perhaps more revolutionary however was Weymann's new double deck body designed for fitting to the recently-introduced rear-engined Leyland Atlantean chassis. This was of lowheight dimensions with an overall height of 13ft. 4in. and was designed jointly by MCCW and Weymann who based it on their Orion and Aurora

Weymann's Aurora body was almost identical to the Orion built by MCCW, thus making their identification extremely difficult. This front entrance 72-seat body on a Guy Arab V chassis of Wolverhampton Corporation was an Aurora built at Weymann's Addlestone factory in 1963.

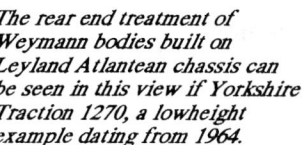
The rear end treatment of Weymann bodies built on Leyland Atlantean chassis can be seen in this view if Yorkshire Traction 1270, a lowheight example dating from 1964.

During 1964/5, Weymann built the lowheight bodies for 50 Dennis Loline IIIs added to the fleet of Aldershot & District. Based on the Aurora design, these were all fitted with a large one-piece sliding door to their front entrance and had seating for 68 passengers. 494KOT, a 1964 example is seen here in NBC days after its transfer to the newly-formed Alder Valley company.

models. With its entrance forward of the front axle and fitted with twin jack-knife doors, the Atlantean body had shallow windows to each deck and featured an almost vertical front. Of its two flat windscreens, that on the offside was angled inward towards its top edge to reduce glare whilst at the rear the body was cut away to allow the bonnet to form a bustle. Seating was provided for 73 passengers and overall, its external appearance was somewhat box-like.

Towards the end of 1959, Weymann completed its first full-height double deck body on a rear-engined chassis when it built a coach version on frames supplied by MCCW for Ribble. Of standard external appearance, this seated 43 passengers in its upper saloon and only 16 in the lower deck where luggage space was incorporated at the rear and in which a servery and toilet was fitted. The prototype for a fleet of similar vehicles for use on Ribble's Lancashire to London services which were launched under the 'Gay Hostess' banner, this vehicle was followed by a production run built by Weymann on its own frames during 1960. From the latter part of that year, the full-height, 14ft. 4in. style of Atlantean body was also made available for normal stage carriage application with seating for 76 passengers.

1960 also saw the construction of 6 special front entrance coach bodies designed jointly by Western Welsh and Weymann and mounted on AEC Reliance chassis. These were loosely-based on the Fanfare design but employed a straight waistrail and used pillars which sloped slightly forward. The stylish D-shaped windows above the front wheel arch were eliminated whilst at the front, peculiar twin windscreens which bulged outwards at their centre were fitted to produce what can only be described as an ugly effect. The front dash panel incorporated two small destination screens, twin headlights, two spot lights and a shallow, wide grille whereas the front roof dome was unglazed and protruded slightly forward of the top edge of the windscreens. Seating was provided for 36 passengers and a further 6 bodies of this style were supplied to Western Welsh in 1961 who named them the 'Cambrian' class.

In 1961, Weymann entered the small bus market with a 30-seat body designed for the Albion Nimbus chassis. This featured the 'big-bus' look by having three conventional sized windows to each side, these having radiused corners and incorporating sliding ventilators while the waistrail stepped downwards at the front. A front entrance with inward-hinged door was placed forward of the front axle, the emergency exit being located at the extreme rear of the offside. Curved windscreens gave the front a pleasing appearance whilst internally, coach-type seats were fitted to allow these vehicles to be used in a dual-purpose role.

A new model, launched at the 1962 Commercial Motor Show, was a 36ft. long single decker of BET styling which continued to use the Hermes name and replaced the previous design bearing this title. Using a straight waistrail which stepped down in the area of the driver's cab, the new Hermes had side windows of generous length with radiused corners and sliding ventilators. The opening portion of the twin windscreens were sloped back towards their top edge whilst a wide entrance, forward of the front axle was protected by twin jack-knife doors. A route number box could be optionally fitted to the curved rear roof dome, below which was a single-piece window and the emergency exit was located at the extreme rear of the offside. Seating

was provided for 53 passengers.

Also making its debut at the 1962 Show was a new Weymann coach body designed as a replacement for the Fanfare. Named the 'Castilian', it had a waistrail which sloped downwards to the rear, vertical pillars between shallow side windows of generous length and twin curved windscreens which sloped back towards their top edge. Both the front and rear roof domes were peaked to protrude beyond the bulkheads and with these modifications, the new coach design was not nearly as attractive as its predecessor.

In 1963, the standard BET-style single deck body was modified to conform to the Group's latest specification and was given double curvature windcreens and rear bulkhead windows above which the roof domes were of the peaked-type. In its new form, the Weymann body was barely distinguishable from those built to the BET design by several other coachbuilders and as an option to having sliding ventilators incorporated into the side windows, forced air ventilation could be specified in conjunction with fixed glazing. Soon afterwards, the double deck body built for fitting to rear-engined chassis was also fitted with BET-style double curvature windscreens and on Daimler Fleetlines, 'shrouds' were fitted at the rear to partly hide the engine bustle and bonnet.

An additional variant of the Aurora-type body was launched in 1964 for fitting to the Dennis Loline III chassis. Being of low-height dimensions, although the usual shallow windows were fitted to the lower deck, those upstairs were of a greater depth and gave the completed vehicle a more pleasing appearance. The front was slightly more vertical than that of the normal lowheight Aurora and featured a full-width Dennis bonnet and grille. The front entrance was fitted with a large, single-piece externally-sliding door while seating was provided for 68 passengers, 39 of whom were accommodated in the upper saloon.

Apart from the Jason II, a revamped ckd single decker produced for the export market, the Loline body was the last new variation to be produced by Weymann, as in 1965 the decision was taken to close the Addlestone factory and transfer all future production to MCCW's Elmdon plant near Birmingham. Before the closure took place however, Weymann built a batch of convertible open top bodies on Daimler Fleetline chassis for Bournemouth Corporation and fitted these with single-piece double curvature windscreens.

As December approached, so the construction of bodies at the Addlestone factory continued as usual and thus when the day of the factory's closure finally arrived, a number of bodies were still in the process of construction. Being unable to complete these - 9 single deck Leyland Leopards for East Midland and and 5 AEC Renowns for Wolverhampton Corporation - they were then transferred to MCCW at Elmdon for finishing.

This then brought to an end yet another era and banished the Weymann name into the annals of history. All production carried out from January 1966 at the MCCW plant at Elmdon carried the latter's name and the only reference remaining to the famous Weymann company was that included in the marketing organisation Metropolitan Cammell Weymann, which continued to be responsible for the sales of all MCCW products.

The final single deck body design to be built by Weymann was to full BET specification and featured peaked front and rear roof domes and double curvature windscreens as illustrated by Maidstone & District AEC Reliance S48 of 1965 vintage.

Built in 1965 for City of Oxford, this single deck body was built to B.E.T. specification.

BUS FAYRE 185

REGIONAL ROUND-UP

After several months of speculation, the battle for Gosport began on 13 October when Red Admiral extended its established 51 service off Bridgemary into Fareham town centre and introduced a new service (numbered 53) between Fareham and Gosport, in effect bringing direct opposition to People's Provincial services 1,2,3,5 & 6 and providing a 5 minute frequency between these two towns. Red Admiral have also made their terminus opposite Fareham bus station and were due to bring their Portsmouth and Emsworth services away from the somewhat remote stands at the other end of town to this same location which is already congested by People's Provincial 'main road' services and half hourly visits by Hampshire Bus on its Winchester to Portsmouth service. Shortly before the introduction of their new services, Red Admiral removed its Fareham 'depot' from within the secure walls of Fort Wallington down into the Fareham Borough Council yard at Broadcut. Although at the moment straws in the wind, rumour is circulating that Admiral is to transfer its Carlyle-bodied Mercedes midibuses to Oxford, although what is to replace them in Hampshire has yet to be established ....

Southampton CityBus has placed in service the first two of its East Lancs single deck-rebodied B35F Atlanteans and has given these new 'dateless' identifications (350/1 OJI1870/1 formerly PCR299M & HTR567P) while 195/6/9/201 (HTR557/65/8/70P) are at present at East Lancs Blackburn factory for similar treatment. Equally as surprising is the acquisition on 2 September of CityBus service 52 (Southampton - Petersfield) by Solent Blue Line as a result of retendering. The surprise here is that CityBus is to continue its operation under franchise to Blue Line with two of that company's Leyland Nationals 428/30 (NEV683M & JNO198N) which have been obtained on indefinate loan for use on this service ! Adding to the surprises from Citybus is the news that Plaxton-bodied Leyland Leopard coach 59 (FEL105L) was raffled at the Netley bus rally (for £1 per ticket). The winner immediately sold this vehicle to the Bournemouth Passenger Transport Association and it is understood that it is to be restored to its original Bournemouth condition at an early date.

Across in the south-east, Kentish Bus are to replace a number of their double deckers operating out of Northfleet garage with new midibuses to leave only 12 double deckers in service from this site. This has angered drivers who, when transferred to the midibuses, will see their wages reduced from £5.40 per hour to £4.35 per hour (phased down over six months) and one cannot help wondering what action they may eventually take in order to protect their earnings. Meanwhile, Kentish Bus has been evaluating a Wadham Stringer Portsdown-bodied Dennis Dart demonstrator on route 12 (River View Park - Gravesend - Northfleet Church) indicating a possible choice for its new midibus fleet.

Maidstone Borough Council has decided that the time has come to sell its bus operating arm, Boro'line, believing that this is in the best interests of the travelling public. In addition, the Council has called for the repeal of the 1985 Transport Act which deregulated bus services, blaming this for much of its current problems. Boro'line will be offered for sale by competitive tender on the open market, although the company's own management will be invited to submit a bid and it would appear that encouragement is being given to buyers that offer existing employees some sort of stake in the future financial success of the company. Who will emerge as Boro'line's new owners is awaited with interest ....

Following the withdrawal of its ex.Ipswich open and closed top Atlanteans and former Blackpool Leyland PD3/11, Eastbourne Buses have decided to replace their cut-down AEC Regent V towing wagon (VSV990, formerly bus no.66) with a Leyland Roadtrain recovery wagon registered A65TBH. New vehicles to join the Eastbourne fleet are 2 Wadham Stringer-bodied Dennis Darts (21/2 - J121/2FUF) and 2 Wadham Stringer Vanguard II-bodied Dennis Javelins (23/4 - J123/4FUF). Of these 22/4 arrived in November while 21/3 will follow early in 1992.

Kent County Council CVE Omnis have been appearing all over the county in recent months with Maidstone & District receiving H395GKO and J110LKO for experimental services in Hawkhurst and Chatham, allocating these temporary fleet numbers 1401/2, and Eastonways of Ramsgate gaining G645EVN which has been transferred from East Surrey. Wealden-Beeline of Five Oaks Green have taken over former Maidstone & District services 200, 211 & 212 in the Tonbridge area and are expected to receive two of Kent County Council's Omnis for these contracted operations. East Surrey have meanwhile been operating a Wadham Stringer Portsdown-bodied Dennis Dart (J556GTP) in cream & blue demonstration livery on local schools contract 651 and on service 303 between Oxted and Redhill.

An interesting move by Brighton Buses has been the rebodying of two Duple-bodied Leyland Leopards with new Willowbrook Warrior bodies. 81 & 85 (UTD203/4T) - formerly 503/4 in the fleet of Southend Transport - have in the process of their transformation been re-registered PIB5144/5 and have both been placed in Brighton's subsidiary Lewes Coaches fleet. On the debit side, Dennis Dominator 40 (JSL281X) has been cannibalised for spares and is now in an advanced state of decay at Lewes Road depot.

The beginning of October marked the increase in frequency of the Brighton to Newhaven service operated by newcomer Haven Coaches of Newhaven. Using their ex.Western Scottish Routemaster (RM933) and former London Buses Fleetline (DM1020), service H2 is now operated on a half- hourly frequency with a newly-introduced hourly extension to Seaford. Responding to this new competition, Brighton & Hove have launched service B1, a weekday 30-minute headway route between Brighton and Newhaven, although the 712 continues unchanged. Brighton & Hove have also placed an order for 150 Almex Eurofare electronic ticket machines which will replace the first generation Almex Timtronic equipment currently used.

Panther Buses of Crawley recommenced the operation of bus services in their own right on 1 October after the expiry of the three-month ban imposed upon them by the Traffic Commissioner, with all their vehicles carrying a large poster in their rear windows declaring 'Panther - Back To Please You Now'. The 'S' prefixes to their service numbers have now reverted to 'P', although it

186 BUS FAYRE

appears possible that the Silverline routes may eventually reappear, thus doubling the number of Panther operated services in Crawley. Such a move would make Panther's fleet as large as that of local rival London & Country, and in preparation for this many more vehicles are expected and additional staff are being recruited. Already Panther has received another ex.London Leyland National (THX188S) which was unusual in that it was delivered already repainted in Panther livery unlike its sisters which still retain their former London colours. Unfortunately however, it has to date seen little service as a result of mechanical problems. Withdrawn and sold are two of Panther's earlier Leyland Nationals, XPR234N and VPT937R.

Guildford and Horsham have until recently been traditionally 'stable' towns for bus services, but like most other places around Britain, have now begun to witness increased competition between the larger concerns and established independents. For many years the former NBC subsidiaries London & Country and Alder Valley co-existed quite happily with independent Tillingbourne with little in the way of competition, but how things are now changing ! The acquisition of Alder Valley by the Drawlane subsidiary, Randomquick in 1990 along with Drawlane's London & Country effectively sandwiched the independent concern with London & Country from 31 August starting the process by diverting its service 425. The Dorking to Guildford route has been diverted from serving Merrow back to its original haunt of Chilworth with a half-hour frequency while Alder Valley West Surrey has introduced an improved 15-minute frequency on its Guildford - Cranleigh services 263/273/283. A further new service - numbered 251 - has been inaugurated between Horsham and North Heath and this competes directly with Tillingbourne's route 51. To respond, Tillingbourne quickly changed its own operations, combining minibus routes 63/73/83 between Guildford and Cranleigh with existing services 23/24 to match Alder Valley West Surrey's 15 minute frequency. A new service (71) provides an hourly response to Alder Valley West Surrey's 251 while another new route (57) links Horsham to Southwater in competition with London & Country's H5 with both the 71 and 57 operating hourly. These changes appear to be only the start of the battle, as all the companies concerned are currently looking for further areas of improvement.

As a result of its Drawlane parentage, Alder Valley have recently transferred several vehicles to London & Country including Leyland Nationals 191/200 and Alexander-bodied Leyland Olympians 906/8/10. All were placed in service with London & Country at its Leatherhead garage still wearing their previous owner's livery, but without fleet names. London & Country have also indirectly acquired an Iveco 49.10 (E976LBK) from W & H Motors of Crawley and have allocated to this, fleet number IMB6 and have also taken into stock a trio of former North Western Carlyle-bodied Freight Rover Sherpa minibuses (D79-81TLV) which are for use on a new Guildford Park and Ride service on Saturdays between Guildford Friary Centre and Artlington Road.

Returning briefly to the south coast, Hampshire Bus has received the first of its new Alexander-bodied Leyland Olympians (220-4 - J620-4GCR) of which 223/4 first operated in Inverness for a short period before travelling south to join their rightful owner. Solent Blue Line are also in the news with their acquisition of a trio of Leyland Nationals from Badgerline (710-2, XEU858-60T), the first of which entered service with Blue Line in full Badgerline livery.

Reading Transport, having acquired Berks & Bucks Londonlink operations from 14 October with at first no changes being made to the timetables, appear to be working towards an operation integrated with their own London services during the spring of 1992. Whilst it is believed that all Berks & Bucks' Jonckheere-bodied Volvo B10Ms (781-90, F771-4/55-60OJH) have passed to Reading with the Londonlink services, the future of one of these coaches must be in doubt following serious accident damage sustained whilst still with its original owner. Berks & Bucks Reading depot at Kenavon Drive has displayed signs offering its lease for sale for several months and it is rumoured that its allocation is soon to be moved to the bus station in Station Hill, Reading in the not too distant future despite this site having no facilities for maintenance, cleaning or refuelling ! Currently, several vehicles are parked behind Kenavon Drive depot marked 'withdrawn' including Leyland Leopards 709/14/6/21/7 (WJM817T, GGM69/72W, APB951X & WPD30Y), the latter of which is still in the blue & white livery of Whites of Baughurst from whom it was acquired some time ago. Reading Transport has meanwhile become the first operator to order Optare's new double decker, the first of which was displayed at the Coach & Bus 91 exhibition at Birmingham in October.

Luton & District has acquired 6 Reeve Burgess-bodied 25-seat Mercedes 709D midibuses from Carlton PSV (dealer) of Rotherham as replacements for a similar number of indestructable Ford Transits at Luton depot. Numbered 6-11 (F121-5/8TRU), these had originally been on lease to Metrobus of Orpington. Of the withdrawn Ford Transits, 21/2/7/9/30 (C21/2NVV, B27HRP, C193/4KBH) have been loaned to Derby City Transport whilst ECW-bodied Leyland Tigers TL8/9/11/28 (TPC108/9/11X, WPH128Y) and Plaxton-bodied Leyland Tigers TP4 & 125 (A104TPA & B287KPF) have been sold to Regal (dealer), Kirkintilloch. Also withdrawn are Leyland Nationals 470/504/21/41 and SNB247 (ORP470M, KNH504N, SBD521R, BVV541T & NPK247R) and Leyland Atlanteans AN157/69/235/871 (VPA157S, XPG169T, JPE235V & MUA871P). Amongst the service changes implemented recently by Luton & District are the introduction of a new hourly service (400) from High Wycombe bus station to Flackwell Heath and a route numbered 502 from Watford to Hemel Hempstead via Hempstead Road, Kings Langley and Two Waters. Operating 4 return journeys on Mondays to Fridays, the latter is designed to compete with Lucketts new 502 service. Further timetable changes were introduced at the end of October covering Hertfordshire County Council tendered services in Watford and Hemel Hempstead while in November changes were implemented in Hitchin, Stevenage and Hemel Hempstead. Meanwhile, Luton & District have now moved out of their depot at Danestreet, Stevenage and into new premises at Norton Green Road in that town, this comprising a fully fenced area with crew, office and refuelling facilities. All Stevenage's maintenance is now being carried out at Hitchin depot which, with Stevenage now forms a single commercial branch of the company.

Chiltern Bus have now been granted planning permission to convert the former Dunlopillo site on Lincoln Road, Cressex into a new depot while Buffalo Travel have commenced operation of two new Bedsfordshire County Council-sponsored services from Luton Centre to a sheltered housing scheme in the Part Town area. Numbered A1 and A2, these operate on Tuesdays and Thursdays, and Wednesdays and Fridays respectively.

Further north, we rather jumped the gun when we stated that PMT had closed its Clough Street, Hanley depot. This is at present still in use although its closure is still very much on the cards.

Greater Manchester Buses have introduced a new livery of orange with black window surrounds and a black skirt (but retaining a white roof) which, in view of the origins of the company's Managing Director, not surprisingly bears slight resemblance to that used by Strathclyde's Buses while Drawlane subsidiary C-Line is at present operating at least one Alder Valley Alexander-bodied Leyland Olympian still in its former operator's livery with the addition of C-Line fleet names.

After months of rumour, it now

appears that Yorkshire Rider are to vacate their Headingley, Leeds depot to allow the site to be sold for redevelopment. Its allocation will then move to Kirkstall works whose engineering functions will be transferred to various of Rider's depots. In a move to prevent PMT launching a new attack on Leeds, Yorkshire Rider have set up a low cost minibus unit under the title of Rider Cubs and have commercially registered the two cross-city routes it had lost to PMT under tender. As a result, PMT have now stated that they will not now be setting up a new subsidiary in Leeds. Rider may yet face a battle however following the setting up of a new company by former AJS Holdings manager, Nigel Jolliffe who has applied for an operators licence to run 12 buses in the south Leeds area under the title 'Quickstep Travel'.

In the north-east, both Go Ahead Northern and Caldaire North East have announced their intention to dispose of all their Leyland National 1s at the earliest opportunity while Northumbria have kept their faith in this model by acquiring several from sister company, Kentish Bus in recent months. New competition in the area is imminently expected from a new operator, Welcome Passenger Services Ltd. of Gateshead who have been granted a 30-vehicle licence. The fleet, which it is believed will be 100% minibus is rumoured to include 10 new Optare Metroriders and 10 Reeve Burgess-bodied Renault S75s although details of the routes to be operated have not yet been publicised. Meanwhile, Go Ahead Northern have ordered 40 9.8m Dennis Darts with Wright 40-seat bodies, the first of which are expected before the end of 1991. Also on order are 14 long wheelbase full-width Optare Metroriders which will be numbered 336-46 (J933-46JJR) and are expected during November for operation from Winlaton depot. Caldaire North East have acquired six more ECW-bodied Bristol VRTs from West Riding/Yorkshire Buses (850/1/65/6/76/9 - YNW292/3S, CWU327T, DWY138/48T, JYG429V) for use in its Tees & District fleet and 3 Plaxton Paramount-bodied Leyland Tigers from Ambassador Travel, Norwich (1409/11/2 - A98)VF, B960/7RVF) for United.

North of the border, the SBG sell-off has been completed with the sale of Western Scottish to its management/employees. Three days after this deal was signed, the company's Clydeside area operations and vehicles were resold to the employees of the old Clydeside company who have commenced operation under the title of Clydeside 2000 which is also being used as the company's fleet name. A revised style of yellow & red livery has also been launched although it will obviously be quite some time before all the fleet is transformed into its new colours.

Across in eastern Scotland, Stagecoach are shortly to vacate their former McLennan premises at Spittalfield and are to reallocate its vehicles to Perth where increased maintenance facilities have been obtained. Further ECW-bodied Leyland Olympians have been received from Bluebird Northern who have also disposed of a number of Alexander-bodied Olympians to Stagecoach-group companies Cumberland and United Counties. These have all been converted from dual to single door layout by Alexander before travelling southwards across the border. Conversely, several of the Leyland Leopards hired by Cumberland to Inverness to assist with the increased operations in that town have now been permanently added to the fleet of Bluebird Northern who themselves have absorbed the Inverness Traction operation.

On the manufacturing front, it is sad to report that Carlyle Bus Centre has now passed into voluntary liquidation with the loss of 160 jobs. For the moment, work at the Carlyle works continues on a much-reduced scale under the supervision of the liquidator and following the receipt of financial support from Dennis and certain finance companies, 6 Darts are being completed for Hong Kong, 10 midibuses for East Kent and a few other sundry vehicles. Although the company's future is extremely uncertain, the liquidator was at the time of writing negotiating with FSV, who bought Dormobile in similar circumstances earlier in 1991, and two other interested parties in an attempt to save the Birmingham-based company from extinction. The Carlyle Bus Parts business is not involved in the liquidation procedure however as it was separated from the Bus Centre last year and will continue to trade normally as the main distributor of parts and service for Van Hool as well as for Carlyle vehicles.

Finally, TT Tsui's Ensign Citybus has launched a new brand name for its LRT tendered operations in Walthamstow. Employing a new yellow livery with a narrow red band below the lower deck windows, the new subsidiary is entitled Walthamstow Citybus but will use Capital Citybus as its fleet name.

Thanks are extended to D.W.Rhodes, J.A.Godwin, R.G.Morrey, A.Parfitt, F.W.York, P.Delaney, Maidstone Borough Council, Northern Group Enthusiasts Club, Cumbria Transport Society, R.Southwell and M.Teale for the provision of news for the above columns. Readers news is always welcome for inclusion in future issues of 'Bus Fayre'.

REVIEWS

PMP BUS WORLD VIDEO - 75 YEARS OF EAST KENT ROAD CAR CO. LTD. £16 post free from PMP, 17 Birchwood Drive, Lower Peover, Knutsford, Cheshire WA16 9QJ. This 90 minute video captures many memories of East Kent as it will always be remembered with its dark red & cream Dennis, Guy and AEC buses and coaches. An hour is spent viewing preserved examples from this fleet and a whole host of buses in the 60s and 70s in everyday service plus a few with subsequent owners, whilst the remaining 30 minutes looks at East Kent in 1991 with its minibuses, Leyland Nationals and MCW Metrobuses etc. A variety of independent operators vehicles are also caught by the camera as are an unbelievable array of almost forgotten makes and models of cars, vans and lorries. Of high quality reproduction, the only improvement which could have been made to this video is a more informed commentary telling viewers where the shots were recorded (not everyone is familiar with Kent and its various bus locations) and a little more about the vehicles filmed and the routes on which they were operating. Do not however let this minor criticism deter you from obtaining this otherwise excellent video.

LIMITED ISSUE BUS PRINTS from World of Transport, 37 Heath Road, Twickenham, Middx. TW1 4AW. £17.95 each or £59.95 for set of 4 (Post paid in UK, £3 per order overseas). These prints from artist Peter Insole (who has exhibited at the Royal Academy) depict four types of London Transport vehicles and each one is a masterpiece. The night shot of trolleybus 1744 captures the atmosphere in and around Ilford on a typically British night (with rain pouring down !) whilst another night scene shows a busy scene in central London in the immediate post World War I period with several B-types in view. The RT age is captured by RTL453 with roof-box body on the 25 service and ofcourse no collection would be complete without the Routemaster, which is represented by a painting of RM1122 in original condition beneath the trolleybus wires on a 281 working to Tolworth. Without doubt, these are some of the best bus paintings your reviewer has ever seen and being 16.5" x 12" are a bargain at £17.95. Only 650 of each print are being produced and each one is numbered and signed by the artist. Packed in a substantial tube, they travel well and are an ideal present for Christmas.

BACK COVER PHOTOGRAPHS

Top : Maidstone Boro'line driver training bus 299 (XKP782A) is a Leyland PD2/3 with Weymann dual-door body. It began life in 1950 with Bournemouth Corporation and was originally registered KEL128.   (D.W.Rhodes)

Centre left : Carrying Weymann front entrance Orion-style bodywork built to the same design as those produced at Elmdon by Metropolitan Cammell Carriage & Wagon Co., Leyland PD3A/1 NNW128R was supplied new to Bournemouth Corporation in 1963 registered 6169RU. It was later sold to Isle of Man National Transport by whom it was re-registered LMN80 and then passed to NAT Holidays, Leeds who used it as a driver training bus, still in Isle of Man livery as seen here.   (K.A.Jenkinson)

Centre right : Liverpool Corporation purchased 100 AEC Regent III's in 1948/9, fitting these with Weymann bodies which were completed by the Corporation in their Edge Lane workshops. One of these buses, A344 (HKF820), which entered service in March 1949 is seen here after being acquired for preservation.

Lower : One of a batch of Leyland KPO3 Cubs bought by London Transport in 1936, 20-seat Weymann-bodied C94 (CLE122) has happily been preserved and is seen here in 1991 after being fully restored in central area red livery. (D.W.Rhodes)

A SPECIAL OFFER TO ADVERTISERS

As a special offer in the January, February & March 1992 issues of 'Bus Fayre', THE FIRST 15 WORDS OF ALL CLASSIFIED ADVERTISEMENTS WILL BE INSERTED FREE. Additioonal words will be charged at 20p each and all adverts must be pre-paid to Autobus Review Publications Ltd., 42 Coniston Avenue, Queensbury, Bradford BD13 2JD. Adverts for inclusion in the January issue (on sale 19 December) must be received no later than 22 November. Box numbers available £2.00

PMP BUS WORLD VIDEOS

TREASURED MOMENTS IN TRANSPORT HISTORY BROUGHT TO YOUR HOME

CELEBRATE 75 YEARS OF EAST KENT ROAD CAR CO. LTD. WITH OUR ANNIVERSARY SPECIAL

Produced with the approval of the operator, this programme starts with over 60 minutes of archive film in full colour stretching back to the days of the Dennis Falcon and Leyland Titan plus of course Guy Arabs. There are plenty of contract liveries, all over adverts and a soundtrack. To complete this feast of nostalgia there is a look at the scene in 1991 where we see the company facing competition on the roads of Kent.
£16 post free

Our comprehensive list contains details of over 50 programmes amongst which is No.23 which contains a medley of archive features including trolleybuses in Derby and Nottingham together with buses in action in Preston, Lincoln and Blackpool, over an hour of vintage film and rounded off with a look at operations in Burton and Warrington today.
£16 post free

Access/Visa welcome

Telephone 0565 722045 (evenings) or write to :
PMP, 17 Birchwood Drive, Lower Peover, Cheshire
WA16 9QJ

JUST IN TIME FOR CHRISTMAS

NEW FROM AUTOBUS REVIEW PUBLICATIONS

BEST BUS

The many changes which have taken place within the Scottish Bus Group between 1985 and 1991 are all recorded in this new book. Covered in the comprehensive text are all the major milestones within this period including the division of the old SBG subsidiaries in 1985, de-regulation in 1986 and the mixed fortunes that followed, the re-merging of companies in 1989 and privatisation in 1991.
Complementing the text are over 200 photographs - a number of which are in colour - which illustrate the wide variety of vehicles and liveries employed by the colourful Scottish Bus Group during its final years.

£8.95
post free

Available from all leading bookshops and enthusiast shops
or direct from
AUTOBUS REVIEW PUBLICATIONS LTD
42 Coniston Avenue, Queensbury, Bradford, BD13 2JD

BUS FAYRE
CLASSIFIED ADVERTISEMENTS

Advertisers are reminded to observe the provisions of the Trades Descriptions Act and the Business Advertisements Disclosures Order when drafting their adverts.

FOR FREE ADVERTISEMENT OFFER SEE PAGE 189 OF THIS ISSUE

FOR SALE

PHOTOGRAPHS OF LONDON BUSES DENNIS DARTS with Reeve Burgess bodies, Westlink Titans, Golden Miller Nationals, Southampton Lynx and Darts. Quality 6" x 4" photos. 32p each + p&p. BusFinders, 35 Gleanings Drive, Norton Tower, Halifax, West Yorkshire HX2 OPA.

WANTED

NEGATIVES, BLACK & WHITE AND COLOUR of buses, trams and trolleybuses present and past. Please send details to Bygone Transport, c/o 42 Coniston Avenue, Queensbury, Bradford BD13 2JD.

BUS FAYRE VOLUME 1 NUMBER 2. Good condition essential. Also Setright ticket rolls : East Kent, London Transport Green Line. Adams, 44 Pennington Place, Tunbridge Wells, Kent TN4 OAQ.

PHOTOGRAPHS OF JXN370. I am urgently seeking colour or black & white photographs of former London Transport RTL47 (JXN370) in service in London, whilst with McLennan of Spittalfield, Scotland and during its period in use with Cransley Farms, Scotland. Can you help please ? Jenkinson, 42 Coniston Avenue, Queensbury, Bradford, BD13 2JD.

SOCIETIES

RIBBLE ENTHUSIASTS CLUB. Monthly bulletin and visits, annual rally, extensive photographs and publications, also secondhand department. Join today and enjoy Ribble country. Details : D.Shaw, Dept B, 8 Millom Close, Rossall, Fleetwood, Lancs FY7 8NU.

WESTERN ENTHUSIASTS CLUB. Keep up to date with all the latest changes in the Western Scottish fleet. Bi-monthly news sheet, tours, visits etc. Details from G.W.Bain, 12 Brisbane Street, Greenock, PA16 8LN.

WANT TO SAVE OLD BUSES ? The British Bus Preservation Group discovers, rescues and restores vehicles, finds storage, supports members restoration projects and keeps an eye on legislation. Members receive a regular newsletter and numerous other benefits. Membership £10 per annum or £6 for unwaged people. To join or for further details write to the BBPG, 109, Wellington Street, Peterborough PE1 5DU. Tel : 0733 898322 or office 0733 237111.

INTERESTED IN CROSVILLE ? Then why not join the Crosville Enthusiasts Club. We publish a monthly 'Review' covering Crosville Wales and the former Crosville Motor Services area and also run tours during the year. For details send large SAE to CEC Secretary, 104 Seaview Road, Liscard, Wirral, Merseyside L45 4LD.

CUMBRIA TRANSPORT SOCIETY through its monthly illustrated newsletter, covers all passenger transport in Cumbria, including Cumberland Motor Services, Shaw Hadwin, minor bus & coach operators, rail, water and air travel. Also visits, trips & slide shows. Details from B.K.Pritchard, 1 Ling Beck Crescent, Seaton, Workington, Cumbria, CA14 1EZ.

VEHICLES FOR SALE

LONDON RT BODY & MECHANICAL SPARES for sale. Numerous parts at reasonable prices. Send details of your requirements. Box S158 Autobus Review Publications Ltd., 42 Coniston Avenue, Queensbury, Bradford, BD13 2JD.

BUS FAYRE - JANUARY 1992
On sale 19 December 1991

This will be a special double size issue containing a wide variety of articles and photographs and several special features. £2.75

PROVINCIAL BUS PROMOTIONS

VISA   ACCESS

1 VICAR PARK ROAD, NORTON TOWER, HALIFAX, WEST YORKSHIRE, HX2 ONL
Telephone : 0422 343557

COLOUR PRINTS ON APPROVAL
Vast range of 6" x 4" prints covering the U.K. from the 1960s to present day. Send 60p for approval list.

DIE CAST MODELS

CORGI

GIFT SETS
East Kent (OB and Regal)	£24.95
Yelloway (OB and Regal)	£24.95
Coventry (Regent and OB)	£20.95
AEC Set (Regent and OB)	£20.95

AEC REGAL COACH
Sheffield United Tours	£12.99
Grey Green	£12.99
Rosslyn Motors	£12.99

METROBUS
Crosville Wales	£7.50
East Kent (B.E.T. livery)	£7.50
Strathclyde	£5.75

CORGI

PLAXTON COACH
East Kent (post deregulation livery)	£8.50
Applebys Coaches	£8.50
Bluebird	£7.50
Scottish Citylink	£7.50

AEC REGENT
City of Oxford	£8.25

EFSI

BOVA FUTURA
Norris of Chatham	£8.95
All-white	£5.50

LLEDO
AEC Renown (Bournvita)	£3.75
AEC Renown (Roses Lime Juice)	£3.75
AEC Renown (Coventry)	£6.25

EFE

HARRINGTON GRENADIER
Black & White	£8.95
Maidstone & District	£8.95

RED RT
Barclays Bank	£5.75
Vernons Pools	£5.75

HORSFIELD TRAM
Leeds	£10.95

All prices include postage & packing. No cheques cashed until model despatched.

We are full time vintage bus owning dealers. We are interested in what we have for sale.
Send large SAE for our advance form and lists. Don't miss out by waiting for models to appear. We can guarantee delivery.